Logan and Cash's Big Day Out

adrienne trzonkowski

Illustrated by: Ashley Delsignore

Logan and Cash's Big Day Out

adrienne trzonkowski

Illustrated by: Ashley Delsignore

AuthorHouse™
1663 Liberty Drive
Bloomington, IN 47403
www.authorhouse.com
Phone: 833-262-8899

Interior Image Credit: Ashley Delsignore

ISBN: 979-8-8230-1143-3 (sc)
979-8-8230-1142-6 (e)

Library of Congress Control Number: 2023912952

Published by AuthorHouse 7/11/2023

authorHOUSE®

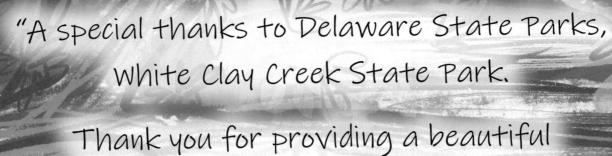

"A special thanks to Delaware State Parks, White Clay Creek State Park.

Thank you for providing a beautiful playground for fur babies past and present.

1

Good morning Logan and Cash.

I love you.

It's going to be a beautiful day.

The sun is out and there is
not a cloud in the sky.

I think we should
go out and play.

Let's pack up some snacks
and plenty of water too.

I think I have an idea
of what we can do.

Let Mama grab your leashes and let mama grab her keys.

I am going to pack up the truck and no Logan, I won't forget the treats.

Ok boys, who wants to go for a ride?
Yes, I said ride!

I can see your tails wiggling, let's go,
I'll help you jump inside.

We are finally here boys.
It's your favorite place.

Momma loves to watch you swim
and all the wildlife you try to chase.

Slow down boys, wait for me, you two run so fast.

I see the trail ahead, and I know you are going to have a blast.

Yippee, we are finally here,
time to cool off and swim.

The water is perfect today,
so shallow and so clear.

Logan, you are such a good swimmer.
Cash, I love to watch you fetch.

You boys are going to be tired.
Later we can rest together
on our favorite bench.

What a perfect day to enjoy the park.
Boys, I know you love this creek.

There is so much to see and do, we
should make this trip every week.

13

Time sure does fly boys,
I think it's time to go.

We have been here for hours and
I bet daddy is getting home.

Don't pout sweet boys,
I hate when you look at me like that.

Today was so much fun,
I promise I'll bring you back.

We are home sweet boys.
It's time to wake up.

I knew from all that swimming and playing you would fall asleep in the truck.

Look boys, daddy is home from work
and I think he has a treat.

Run boys, go get him,
I'll let you off your leash.

19

Logan and Cash, it's getting late.
I think its time for bed.
You boys had a big day
and remember what I said?

Momma knows you love to go to the park,
and she promises to bring you back.

She loves to see you smile,
she loves to see you play.
She loves to see your tails wiggle,
and she can't wait for another sunny day.

These days spent together at the park
are memories being made.
Memories she will look back on
and smile at one day.

21

Good night
Logan and Cash.

I love you.

22

In loving memory of Logan and Cash.
2005-2021/2022

Life because of you was a blessing.
Life without you is a beautiful memory.

Professional photo taken by

Brittany Elena Photography

Printed in the United States
by Baker & Taylor Publisher Services